ZEN
AND THE
ART OF
STICKFIGHTING

STEPHEN F. KAUFMAN
HANSHI, 10TH DAN

CB
CONTEMPORARY BOOKS

Library of Congress Cataloging-in-Publication Data

Kaufman, Stephen, 1939–
    Zen and the art of stickfighting / Stephen F. Kaufman.
       p.   cm.
   ISBN 0-8092-2585-9
    1. Stick fighting.   2. Zen Buddhism and martial arts.
I. Title.
GV1141.K38   2000
796.8—dc21   99-29713
                                      CIP

*This book would not have been possible
without the generous support of
David and Marietta Teitler*

Cover design by Todd Petersen
Cover and interior photography by Battman-NYC
Interior design by Hespenheide Design

Published by Contemporary Books
A division of NTC/Contemporary Publishing Group, Inc.
4255 West Touhy Avenue, Lincolnwood (Chicago), Illinois 60712-1975 U.S.A.
Copyright © 2000 by Stephen F. Kaufman
Printed in the United States of America
International Standard Book Number: 0-8092-2585-9

00 01 02 03 04 05 VL 18 17 16 15 14 13 12 11 10 9 8 7 6 5 4 3 2 1

Contents

Acknowledgments

Many people have been instrumental in the development of this book. I would like to express my thanks to the following people.

Nicolas H. Ekstrom
Paul Insalaco
Lianne Johnson
Lita Kaufman
Jason Levine
Hitomi Sayabashi
Steven Shenouda

Introduction

Zen and the Art of Stickfighting is a book for anyone who wants to learn to defend him- or herself with a walking stick, cane, or umbrella. This book will teach you to wield a stick properly, starting with selection of a stick, the correct grips and prescribed methodology, and how to use the techniques for maximum effect with minimum effort. Personal results will depend upon the amount of study and practice you put into acquiring these new skills. The student's physical condition may present some limitations, but these reasons alone should not deter anyone with a sincere desire to learn. Stickfighting can be mastered by anyone with the diligence to acquire the necessary skills.

The realistic and functional Zen attitudes of *attack/no-attack* and *going into the attack* are stressed. These ideas focus on the evolution of overall interactive strategies used by real-life warriors since time immemorial, and how such warriors have been helped by these ideas to overcome shortcomings in their lives. When you become familiar with these principles, along with the accompanying techniques, you will be able to deal with *any* situation, not only physically, but mentally as well.

The significant advantage of a stick, cane, or umbrella as a self-defense device is its fundamental legality. Carrying a walking stick does not represent an intentional weapon, assuming that it doesn't look like a cudgel. We live in a society that seeks to protect the rights of victims, but it is the individual's responsibility to defend him- or herself. Walking sticks, canes, and umbrellas afford this protection and are easier to wield than exotic devices such as Phillipine *escrima* sticks or *spring batons*. A "stick" is already "out" and does not have to be drawn. It should be noted that the stick or cane you select must not be the type that conceals a sword or blade in the shaft. These are considered to be concealed weapons, and they are illegal. They are intrinsically weak because of the break in their structure and as a rule are not dependable.

The techniques in this book are real and can seriously harm someone. The use of them is not to be taken lightly nor should they be used indiscriminately. It is highly recommended that adults supervise the training of children, explaining to them the responsibility of having this knowledge. Also, the reader will observe that certain movements are executed by the models in less than perfect form. This is because this level of stickfighting is intended for practical self-defense and is therefore being demonstrated by people without formal training. You should not think that if you are imperfect in form you will not be effective. You will be if you observe the principles being taught.

As a result of your practice, a *personalized* self-defense system will develop. Stickfighting should not be considered an ethnic art that belongs to any specific culture. A stick can be wielded as effectively as a Japanese *Bo*, Philippine bamboo sticks, or a Brooklyn stickball bat. When you learn the proper manner in which to wield a stick, you will also come to understand what you are doing as universal in scope and a perfectly reasonable way to defend yourself. The strategy and tactics you will learn from this book represent logical and efficient ways to deal with a confrontation. It would be impossible to list and demonstrate every combination. Those shown are considered to be effective by most masters. When you learn the art, you will add preferences to your repertoire.

No special physical conditioning is required, but a simple warm-up routine is suggested to loosen your limbs and get your blood flowing. It should be done before practice sessions and any intense exercising. Also, it is prudent to wear protective equipment during practice sessions with a partner. Getting whacked over the head with a stick, even softly, hurts. Study the pictures carefully. Imitate the positions and forms to the best of your ability while taking care not to hurt or strain yourself, especially if you are using dormant muscles. When you find yourself tiring, it is wise to stop and let your body acclimate itself.

Much repetition is used throughout the text to enforce the main ideas that lead to proficiency and effectiveness. Other than that, there is no profound philosophy in this book. The "Zen Tips" are specific to what you are learning and will benefit you in your studies. Take them to heart, think them through, and heed the advice they reveal. You will find that Zen thinking is simply an awareness of yourself and your environment as *un*common sense. Think about what you are doing. Study and master *Zen and the Art of Stickfighting*.

Stephen F. Kaufman, Hanshi
New York

PART I

Fundamentals

1

Selecting a Stick

Walking sticks, canes, and umbrellas come in different shapes and sizes depending on ornamentation. To train properly, a plain stick is recommended. Get one that is easy to wield with one hand; therefore, optimal weight and length should be your objective. The length should be between twenty-eight and forty inches, depending upon your height, measured from the floor to slightly below your hip. The weight, neither heavy nor light, is your choice. Maneuverability and comfort in handling should be your prime concern. When you have developed the proper skills, you can train with a heavy club to increase muscle tone and bodily strength but not in the beginning.

ZEN TIP

Do not select a stick made of two parts. Weakness at the joint can cause it to break when applying a powerful strike.

A good stick can be selected at any lumber-yard. Maple, briar, thornwood, ash, or any durable hardwood is desirable. Regardless of length, it should balance easily in the middle, halfway between both ends. The width depends on what feels comfortable in your hand, usually $3/4$ to $1^{1}/2$ inches. You can find additional choices in any martial arts catalog, and there are shops that sell one-piece walking sticks. Medical supply houses offer a variety of canes, but select one made of wood, which has a more natural feel than metal or Lucite. A sawed-off broom handle can also be used. If you choose an umbrella, it should be of one piece and not the telescoping type.

Keep in mind that you do not want your stick to appear to be a weapon nor to suggest any form of potential violence. The police can stop you, it can be confiscated, and you could be subject to a fine and arrest.

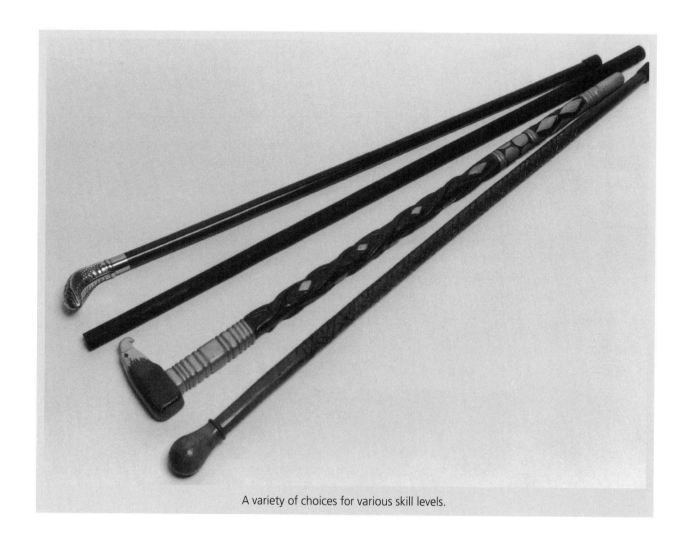

A variety of choices for various skill levels.

Multiple-joint weak point.

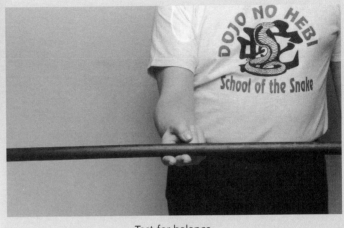

Test for balance.

Your choice should not have any protuber-ances, extensions, or adornments to interfere with the balance. Save fancy designs for the walking stick that you will carry in the street when your skills are under control. For now, consider maneuverability and ease of use as the main reasons for selection. A sawed-off broom handle is naturally balanced and will permit you to develop the required flexibility needed during practice sessions. It is not necessary for the stick to be tapered at either end. When you execute a thrust or a jab, the taper will not make much difference when proper technique is executed.

ZEN TIP

The less obvious you are, the more effective you can be.

2

The Correct Grip

A correct grip must be mastered at the outset of training if you expect to be proficient. Although this may seem obvious, some people find it awkward to maintain a proper grip in the beginning, and because they are lazy, they negate their own effectiveness. If you find the stick difficult to control, rethink your objective with more determination, knowing you will succeed. Doing so will enable you to wield the stick with authority, good technique, and control. Make the decision to wield it correctly from the start.

ZEN TIP

Hold the stick properly in the beginning, so you won't have to correct bad habits later on.

ONE-HAND GRIP

Grip the stick with the small, ring, and middle fingers while applying firm pressure. Holding the stick in such a manner enables you to control the whipping action of your wrist when striking a target. The forefinger lends additional support and maneuverability, while the thumb, resting in a natural position, gives balance to the grip and facilitates aim. This is the proper way to hold the stick and is the most effective way to develop authority in the application of technique. Hold the stick approximately 1½ fist-widths from the end and practice the grip with both left and right hands.

HOLDING THE STICK CORRECTLY WITH ONE HAND

Three-finger grip.

Proper grip and distance of the hand from the end of the stick.

ZEN TIP

A proper grip permits the wrist to remain flexible and enables a whipping action to develop on delivery of the strike.

TWO-HAND GRIP

For two-hand strikes, place the second hand in front of the first as you would a baseball bat or a golf club. The same rule applies with small-, ring-, and middle-finger control. You will be applying techniques in multiple directions and will be using the two-handed technique for situations where the hands must be kept apart. Train yourself to manipulate the stick with left-over-right and right-over-left two-hand grips.

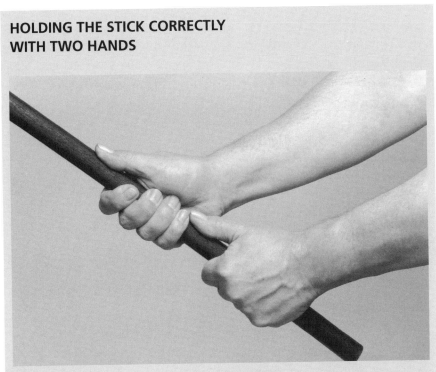

HOLDING THE STICK CORRECTLY WITH TWO HANDS

Close two-hand grip.

Wide two-hand grip, form one.

Wide two-hand grip, form two.

WRIST FLEXIBILITY

To become proficient in the application of correct strikes, it is necessary to strengthen the wrists. Twirling exercises are used to accomplish this. They are easy to perform and are essential in many attacking techniques.

Hold the stick extended in either hand. Maintain the correct grip and make small figure eights, gradually enlarging the area of the figure. Do this in both directions and until the stick feels comfortable in both the left and right hands. Eventually, you may want to increase the weight of the stick to further strengthen your wrists. You will find the delivery of strikes much easier to master if you take the time to develop flexibility in your wrists at the beginning of training.

ZEN TIP

Practice figure eights with the two-hand grip in both directions.

Stick Control and Switching Hands

3

There is always the possibility that you will be unable to use your favored hand to strike a blow during an attack. For this reason it is important to become functional with switching the stick back and forth between both hands. Switching hands should be done as a smooth transition with either one- or two-hand technique regardless of the direction or target that is under attack. Ideally, changing hands should be executed in a subtle and unnoticeable fashion. This comes in time, and you will further appreciate your skills once you can do this.

ZEN TIP

Smoothness of motion is essential for the proper application of strikes.

BASIC SWITCH

Holding the stick in either hand, swing it side to side and up and down. During the motion, switch hands and continue to strike in the same direction. As an example, an outside strike becomes a reverse strike. Maintain the proper grip and keep your wrists straight.

ZEN TIP

Let the switching be as extensions of the hand.

Switch start.

Switch in progress.

Switch completed.

FIGURE-EIGHT SWITCHING

Swing the stick in a figure-eight pattern, first left to right and then right to left. Do this with both hands.

ONE HAND TO TWO HANDS AND BACK AGAIN

Switch from one hand to one hand and then to two hands. Do these in all directions— over, under, left, and right—until you are comfortable and the changes are smooth. Practice switching from one hand to two hands and from two hands back to one hand.

VARIATIONS IN SWITCHING

Changing directions in the midst of a strike gives you flexibility. Switch hands overhead to underhand, side to overhead, and underhand to backswing while practicing. When you think you are ready, invent your own, but keep them strictly practical. Practice the following.

1. Right underhand to left middle outside
2. Left overhead to right bottom
3. Right thrust to left middle outside
4. Right outside to left thrust
5. Left bottom to right thrust
6. Right overhead to left overhead
7. Left outside middle to right outside middle
8. Right bottom to left outside middle

ZEN TIP

When executing a strike, breathe in and breathe out naturally.

ZEN TIP

Switches should be done with smoothness and subtlety.

4

Stepping and Shifting

If you do not step and shift correctly, you will lose balance and be unable to execute proper technique. As an example, it is never wise to cross your feet—with the exception, perhaps, of covering only a slight move to either side. When it is necessary to cover large distances, it is best to face into the direction you are going and simply move forward. In close combat it is better to move short distances by shifting and sliding in the direction you wish to go. Correct balance is maintained by keeping your stance comfortable and your feet rooted to the ground. If you feel awkward, change body position. Shifting and stepping should be done as follows.

ZEN TIP

When moving from side to side, use your outer foot to propel you in the opposite direction.

SHIFTING

The outer foot propels you in the direction you want to go—left or right.

As you develop synchrony of motion, a natural harmony will develop in your body, mind, and spirit. An ability to

To left.

overcome adverse situations will start to become evident.

Moving forward and back is done in the same manner. Use your rear foot to propel you forward. Use your front foot to propel you backward. Consider the distance you have to move.

To right.

STEPPING

Stepping is simply the act of moving in or out with quick steps to the left or right. When stepping laterally, always place your outside foot behind the one remaining stationary.

ZEN TIP

Step lightly, and regardless of direction, don't trip over yourself.

Sidestepping to the right.

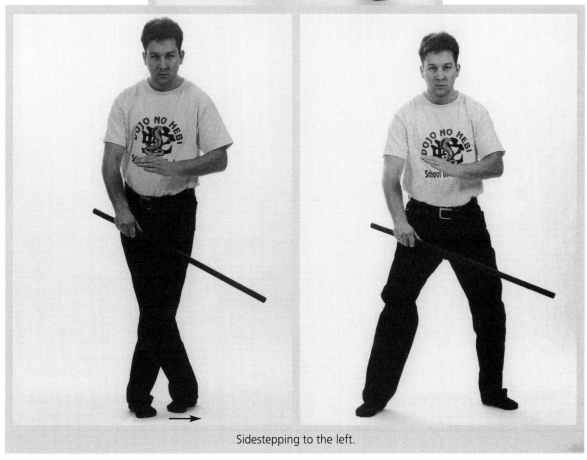

Sidestepping to the left.

5

Directions of Attack and Vital Striking Points

There are an infinite number of points available to hit when attacking a target, but you should focus only on the ones shown in this chapter. These "directions" also contain vital striking points. Developing technique in various directions will give you the freedom to strike at any target with productive focus. Endeavor to gain control of each direction of attack along with the flexibility needed to change direction when required. Anything other than these directions is only a variation and all points can be attacked with one hand or two, using over, under, left, and right strikes and the thrust. There are no other directions to attack regardless of clever technique.

ZEN TIP

Clever techniques should be avoided. They give you a false sense of security. The resultant arrogance will betray you.

TARGET DIRECTIONS AND HIT POINTS

For each type of strike shown in this book, the following areas are effective targets:

> Top of head
> Shoulders, neck, or side of head
> Arms, legs, or ribs
> Knees
> Groin
> Eyes, throat, chest, or abdomen

Practice with the idea of striking in a straight line. You will develop an advantage with the ability to control your actions from any direction—front, side, or back—without becoming sloppy during execution. When you attack with proper striking technique, you will have no difficulty in delivering stunning and effective blows.

ZEN TIP

Striking vital points can inflict severe damage and pain.

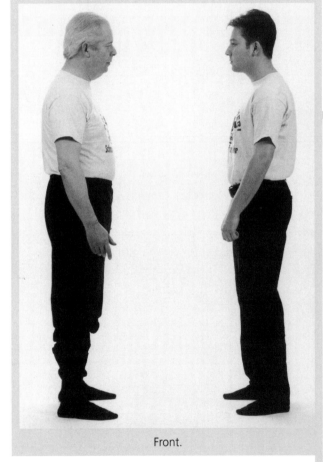

Front.

Side.

VARIATIONS OF ATTACK POSITIONS

Face-to-face with a target is not the only way to attack. You can attack from behind and from either side. Also, the attacker him- or herself can be in attack mode or not.

Striking a target from behind is a reality. You cannot predetermine where you will strike an enemy during a conflict. Training prepares you to do the right thing at the right time.

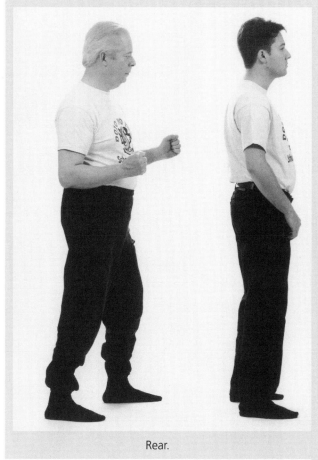

Rear.

Back to back.

Off-Balance Strikes

In combat, the possibility of being off balance is real. For additional competency, practice all techniques while standing on either foot.

In a physical confrontation, you must not consider the feelings of the person or persons you are defending against. Obviously, your attackers are not concerned about you and it is detrimental to your health and safety to be overly concerned for them. Think this through if it is unclear in your mind.

Any target you strike is valid when delivering forceful blows. Strikes are made more effective when a vital spot is hit. In training and practice, proper form and balance will determine your ability to strike any target with ease and effectiveness. The attacker's head should not be considered any more important than the ankles or the knees. The wrist is also an excellent target when you strike properly.

Keep in mind the reason you are practicing: to be able to stave off an attack. Do what is necessary to protect yourself and escape from harm's way. Sometimes it is required that you counterattack the eyes or throat, and you should not hesitate to do so. A jab to the instep is most effective as well. When you become familiar with the targets and hit points, you will come to understand the value of form and balance.

ZEN TIP

Training to execute proper technique when off balance will give you an edge when it is necessary to attack from an unorthodox position.

Front off-balance strike to the legs.

Front thrust on one foot.

6

How to Think of Attacks

GOING INTO THE ATTACK

As specific techniques are developed, you will be constantly reminded to *go into the attack*, which means commitment to the attack. This is sound thinking. With continued practice, you will come to see the reasoning behind it, and it will become evident as you proceed through *Zen and the Art of Stickfighting*. Though this concept may sound alien, perhaps because of a natural reaction to flinch or to move away from an attack, it is, however, an essential attitude. To understand this mentality takes thought and practice. It is not to be confused with rushing headlong into an overwhelming situation.

> ## ZEN TIP
>
> *The mentality of going into the attack suggests commitment to what you are doing. Your actions should be done with resoluteness—or not at all.*

ATTACKING THE ATTACK

In practice, consider that you *attack the attack* rather than the attacker, and come to understand that the function of the target is to accept your actions as an extension of its own being. Though this may seem *way out* at this point in your training, the reality is that you will be empowered to alleviate the fear of thinking that you are overwhelmed by an attacker's size, bravado, or the weapon being employed against you. This idea will become clear as you progress, and the sound thinking behind it will become apparent.

ATTACK/NO-ATTACK

The Zen concept of *attack/no-attack* should be used in and through your life without having to think about it. It simply means that you should be on your guard and prepared to act without becoming paranoid, while at the same time remaining calm. Training provides you with the ability to act or react: knowing when and when not to do something. It is necessary to practice for the mind and the body to be able to act and react on the physical level, automatically, when it is necessary; and so you should always practice to hone your skills. Without spending countless hours in meditation, accept accomplishment of a goal as "already done," and you will experience it as such.

To develop the proper attitude of already done, and to believe it, you should not be nonchalant about the idea and expect it to

be there when you want it without conscious training. You want the attitude to be permanent; it is a prerequisite to being competent.

THE ATTITUDE OF GOING FORWARD

In stickfighting, as in anything else, you must think in terms of succeeding in your endeavor. If you don't think in these terms, you can struggle for years and never arrive at a level of competency that you will respect. Leaving things to chance will keep you from deriving the joy and pleasure from any activity you are involved with. The *attitude of going forward* should be evident in every aspect of your life. Once you accept this attitude, you will never "lose" at anything. There will be no reason to because of the confidence you develop. Also, if you are "in close," meaning you are in your attacker's face, it is very difficult for the attacker to complete any strikes against you. You will see this more thoroughly as you proceed.

As you practice the techniques in the following sections, keep in mind that the reason you are practicing is to be able to defend yourself with a minimum of risk. To do this properly, it is necessary to put your whole self into the act whether you consider your actions practice or anything else. Miyamoto Musashi, one of Japan's greatest warriors, said, "You can only fight in battles the way you practice in training." This is very obvious and very true. If you fool around during practice, you will never have the right attitude to employ your skills should the need arise.

When executing technique, put your heart into it. A benefit to this type of training and thinking is that you will recognize other situations or challenges in your life and deal with them accordingly. In the following pictures, determine the difference in the strictly defensive mode compared to one where the defender is going in to meet the enemy. Develop the confidence needed to carry through and complete the act.

An insecure approach and strike.

Attacking with confidence.

PART II

Technique Development

7

The Basic Warm-Up

It is important to keep the body flexible and stress free at all times. A well-tuned, well-toned body gives you an overall feeling of confidence for success in all that you do. It is easily arrived at with a simple warm-up routine, which you should do upon arising in the morning, or at any time during the day, whether or not you are going to practice the art of stickfighting. It is not necessary, for the purposes of this training, to do much more than is shown in the following pages unless you have a specific desire to do so.

ZEN TIP

You are the image you present to the world and to yourself.

Incorrect posture during breathing.

Correct posture during breathing.

BREATHING

There is more to breathing than a mechanical action if you use it correctly. Proper breathing supplies the body with the right amount of oxygen and keeps your organs functioning correctly. Air should be taken into the abdomen and exhaled when you are done with it. Though this may seem obvious, most people prefer to keep air locked inside of their chests when they make exerting moves, forcing themselves to strain when executing anything. Chest breathing does not provide adequate circulation.

Concentrate on breathing into the abdomen and exhaling with slight force during exertion. To develop deep breathing in the abdomen, think in terms of breathing into your groin. Obviously you cannot really do this, but the idea is to develop an attitude of breathing deeply. Try it.

Breathing should be done slowly and calmly. When you breathe hard and fast, you run the risk of hyperventilating, which can cause dizziness and loss of balance. When you are short of breath, relax and breathe deeply a few times to calm the body. Posture also has a lot to do with breathing properly. Endeavor not to hunch your back as shown in the photograph at the top of the page.

ZEN TIP

Breathe deeply and think in terms of relaxation.

ARMS AND THE UPPER BODY

Reaching Up and Out

Stand with your feet approximately 1 1/2 body-widths apart, and breathe deeply, filling your abdomen with air. Stretch your arms up to the ceiling, slowly, while exhaling. Gently lower your arms in front while breathing in and out. Do it again, but this time stretch your arms to the opposite walls, exhaling during the movement.

REACHING AND STRETCHING OUT

Reaching out and stretching arms to the side.

FORWARD AND REVERSE ROTATIONS TO LOOSEN THE SHOULDERS

Forward and reverse rotations.

Stretching should make you feel good. Relax for a moment, and then do the exercises again, this time stretching to the side even farther than before. Do the same thing when reaching forward. With your arms out to the side or in front, make circle movements forward and back. Loosen up completely by repeating each motion until you are comfortable.

Bending from Side to Side and Front to Back

With hands on hips, lean to the left and then lean your body to the other side. Do not strain yourself by going past your natural point of balance. This exercise will enable you to stretch farther each time. Get your body used to doing something it may not have done in a long time. Keep your legs straight and feel your muscles stretching. Be careful and keep in mind that damaged mus-

cles will cause you to wait until they are healed before you can comfortably continue. Do things the easy way.

BENDING SIDE TO SIDE AND FORWARD TO BACK

Bending to the right and left.

Bending forward may cause you to lose balance. It is a good idea to have your hands in front of you to protect you from falling forward. When bending backward, have your hands on your buttocks to support your back. Don't forget to exhale during exertion.

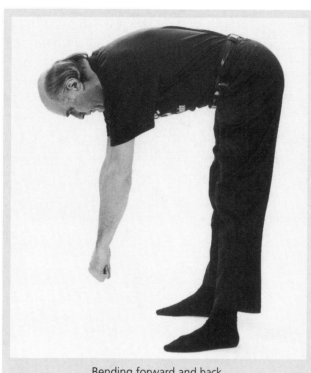

Bending forward and back.

Arms Over and Under While Twisting

Cross your arms over and under while twisting your body to the left and then to the right.

The entire upper torso warm-up should take no more than two minutes.

LEGS AND THE LOWER BODY

Knee Bends and Knee Raises

Knee bends should be done cautiously and slowly. While holding onto a chair, lower your body, making sure not to strain any muscles. Stay on your toes or be flat-footed, whichever is more comfortable for you. If you feel any pain, stop immediately and rise up. Lift your legs one at a time, gently shaking them to relieve any tension.

Continuing with this exercise will soon give you the control you need. Don't be surprised or be nervous if you hear clicks and pops coming from the joints. You may not have exercised for a long time, and this is your body's way of letting you know. Take it easy and go slowly. When you are in the bent position, spread your legs apart, gently. Stretch in and out and breathe deeply.

ZEN TIP

In the beginning, hold the back of a chair for balance when doing leg exercises. This will keep you from falling and losing confidence.

ARMS OVER AND UNDER WITH TWIST

To the right.

To the left.

BENDING AND STRETCHING
THE LEGS AND INNER THIGHS

Knee bend with chair.

Spread legs in bent position.

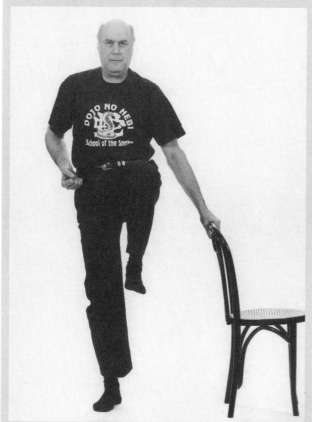

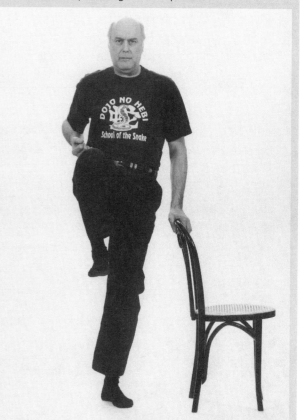

Knee raises, left and right.

Leg Swings

This exercise will warm up and loosen your leg muscles. Gently swing each leg back and forth while keeping them as straight as possible. Hold the back of a chair when you first start.

Swinging leg forward.

Swinging leg backward.

Calf Raises

Hold the back of a chair. Carefully and slowly raise your body.

You have just gone through a simple warm-up. Some of you may wish to increase the amount of time and the type of exercise. Do whatever makes you happy. What you have just done is adequate for the purposes intended. Exercise with spirit, and use correct breathing. After you have completed the warm-up, take a rest.

It is always best to follow the instructions in the order they are presented. Do the warm-up exercises as indicated, making changes only where you feel they are personally necessary. And remember, just because you think you are in condition does not mean that you are.

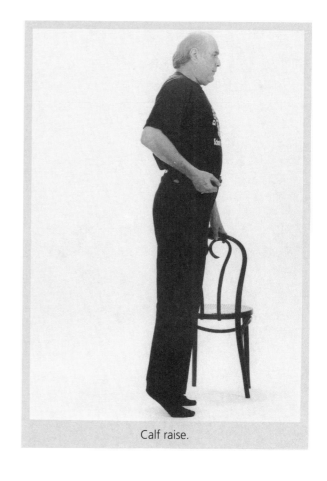

Calf raise.

8

Forward Strikes and Attacks

Rushing through the learning stages of anything will cause the value of your study to be minimized and, as a result, your efforts will be mediocre regardless of appearances of technique. Working slowly enables you to understand what you are trying to accomplish as well as develop physical skill. Learn the simple techniques before attempting the advanced ones if you want to execute proper technique. It is imperative that you control what you are doing to be effective. Practice the strike and get comfortable with it before practicing the attacks.

There are infinite combinations that can be used with a stick, cane, or umbrella, but it is not possible to list and demonstrate all of them. The techniques in this book are practical and will serve your purposes when you understand them. Before attempting to develop your skills, certain things must be taken into consideration, which will help you develop more quickly and with intelligent effectiveness.

ZEN TIP

Make haste slowly.

THE IMPORTANCE OF A STRAIGHT WRIST

The wrist must be kept straight until the instant prior to contact, at which time a whipping motion is employed as if you were casting a fishing rod. The snap enables you to penetrate the target with deliberation instead of wildly swinging at the target out of fear or ignorance.

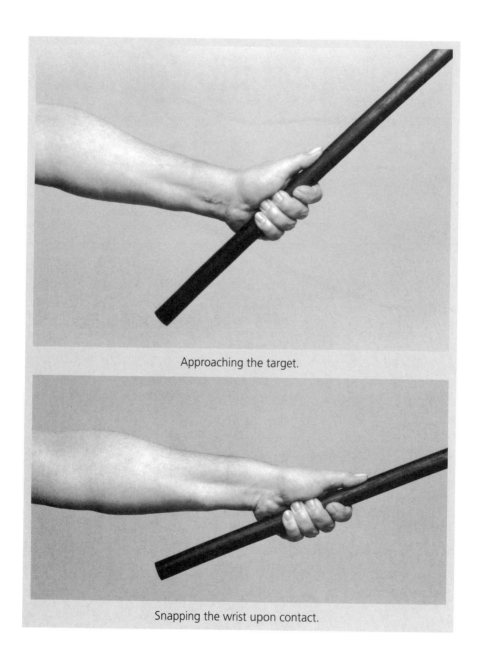

Approaching the target.

Snapping the wrist upon contact.

CUTTING THROUGH

When delivering a strike, it is important to think in terms of *cutting through* the target rather than slashing at it. In keeping with Zen wisdom, it is always wiser to penetrate with authority and conviction rather than to try and hit the target in a haphazard manner.

Improper strike approach causes slashing.

Proper striking technique—*cutting through*.

BALANCE

Effective penetration of a target requires proper balance in addition to commitment and intent. Do not lean to the side unnecessarily. Bending too far forward, backward, or to the side will throw your balance off center. When maintaining balance, keep your spine as straight as possible and your head up.

Improper balance.

Proper balance.

STRIKES AND ATTACKS

Forward Thrust

Point the stick at the target and stab with an attitude of penetration. Clench fist when striking.

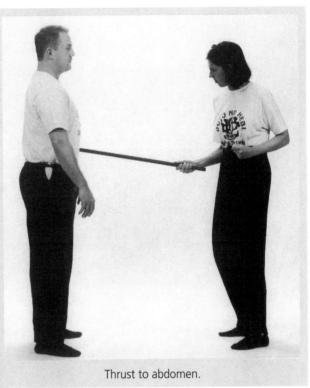

Thrust to abdomen.

STRIKES

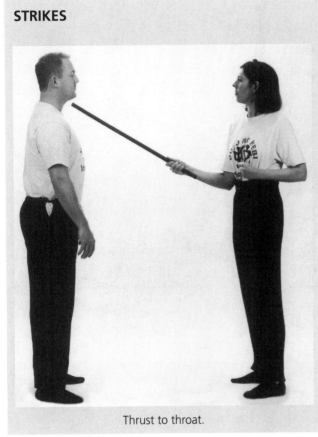

Thrust to throat.

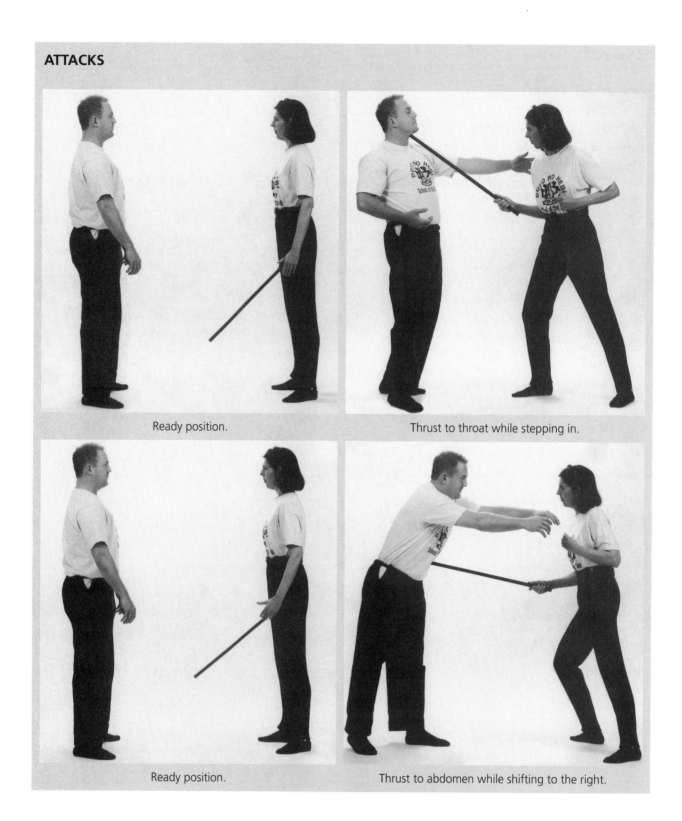

Ready position.

Thrust to throat while stepping in.

Ready position.

Thrust to abdomen while shifting to the right.

ZEN TIP

Practice each move as if it were an actual attack.

Practicing technique as an attack puts the action into the proper perspective. Step forward and practice striking each of the targets, then practice the same strikes while stepping back and shifting to the right and left. In this manner you will come to understand many of the possibilities involved with any particular technique. Make it your goal to master each of the techniques by practicing them in all variations while switching hands. If you take the time to do this now, your techniques will be more efficient and effective.

Front Overhead Strike

Bring the stick over your shoulder and strike down quickly. The target is the head and shoulders.

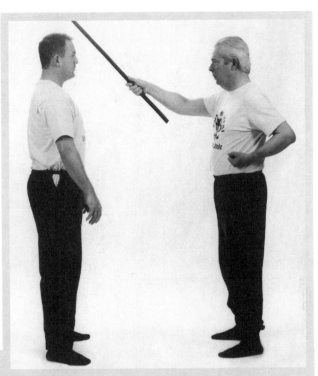

Overhead strike.

STRIKES

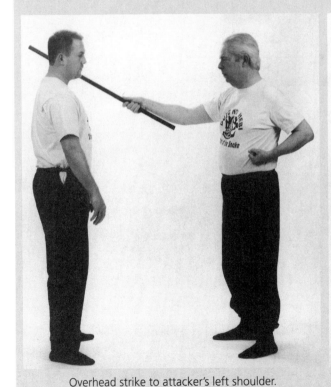

Overhead strike to attacker's left shoulder.

Overhead strike to attacker's right shoulder.

Ready position.

Overhead strike while shifting to the right.

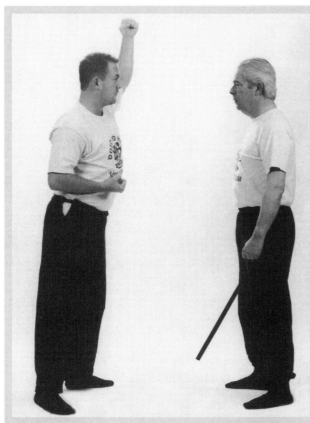

Ready position.

Left shoulder strike while stepping in.

Ready position.

Right shoulder strike with two hands while stepping back.

Front Rising Strikes

Holding the stick at your side, snap the wrist in an upward motion as the arm rises. Use this attack against the groin and the jaw.

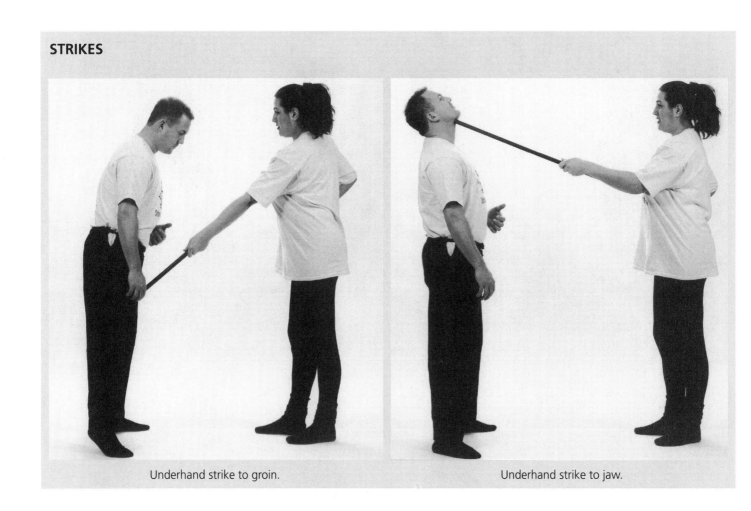

STRIKES

Underhand strike to groin.

Underhand strike to jaw.

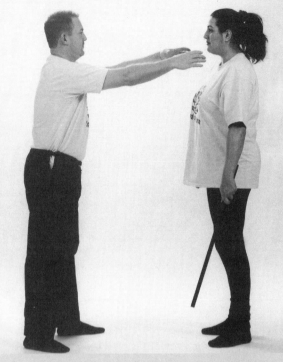

Ready position.

Underhand strike to groin while stepping in.

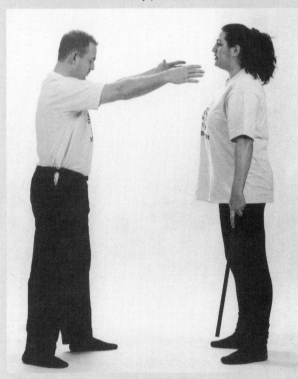

Ready position.

Underhand jaw strike while shifting right and switching hands.

Front Outside Strike

This is used to attack the head, ribs, arms, and legs.

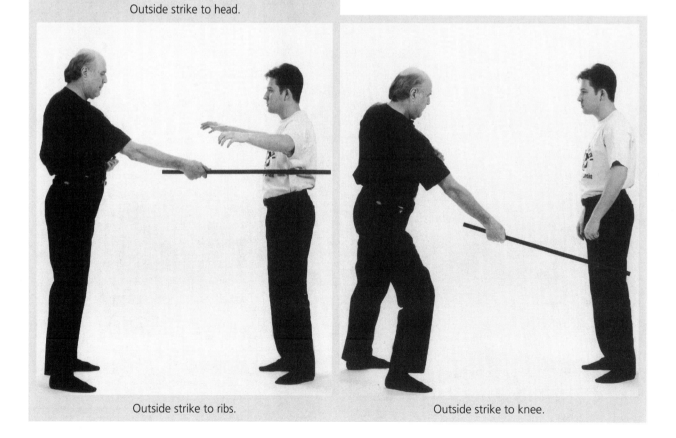

Outside strike to head.

Outside strike to ribs.

Outside strike to knee.

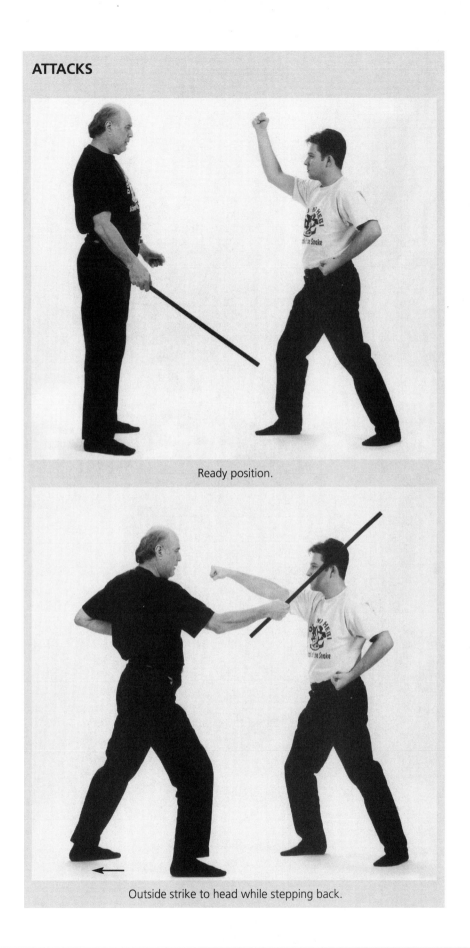

Ready position.

Outside strike to head while stepping back.

Ready position.

Switching hands and stepping in.

Outside strike to ribs.

ATTACKS (continued)

Ready position.

Outside strike to knee while shifting left.

Front Reverse Strike

This is the opposite of the previous strike and attacks the same targets.

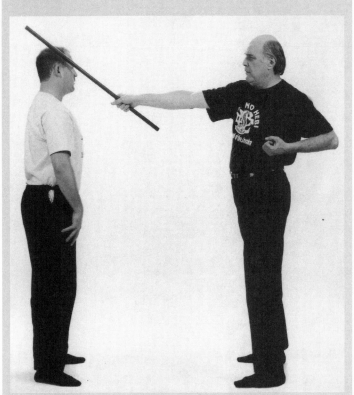

Reverse strike to head.

Reverse strike to ribs.

Reverse strike to knee.

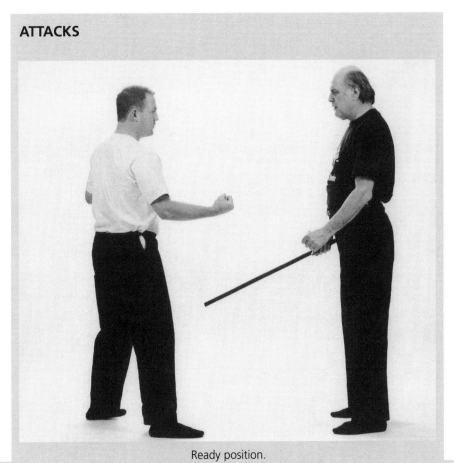

Ready position.

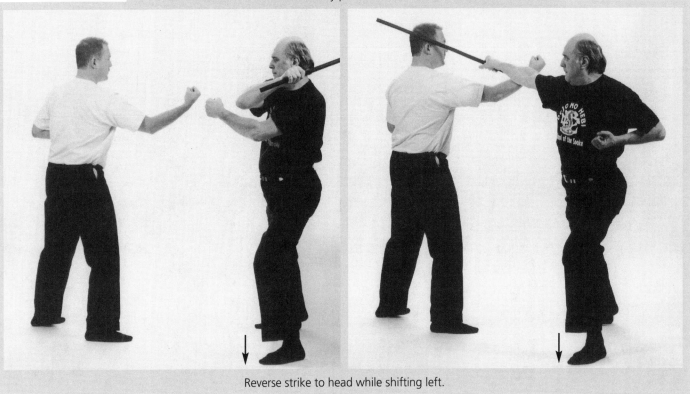

Reverse strike to head while shifting left.

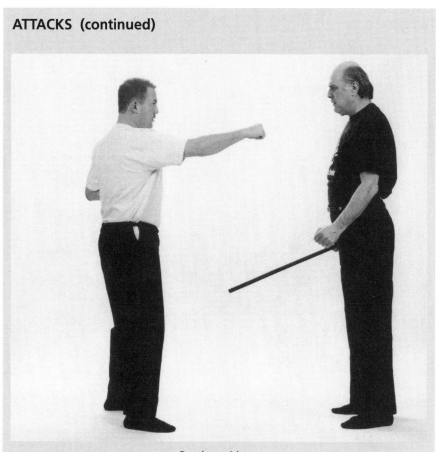

Ready position.

Reverse strike to ribs while stepping in.

Ready position.

Reverse strike to knee while stepping in.

These are the forward strikes and attacks you should use regardless of the target you are attacking. Everything else is a variation, which you can personally develop once you understand the basic idea of a counterattack. Correct form and balance are required to produce effective and efficient strikes. Remember to practice counterattacks with left-, right-, and two-hand techniques. Utilize stepping and shifting in, out, and to the side. Maintain the attitude of cutting through the target while going into the attack. (Read my *Martial Artist's Book of Five Rings* to gain an increased understanding of cutting through as well as other combat strategies.)

Practice until you are aware of the possibilities of strikes and counterattacks. You will be able to defend yourself regardless of circumstance and will develop correct balance to strike at a target from any direction.

9

Side Strikes and Attacks

The main emphasis in a counterattack should be on striking the target. Side strikes are often used, and you should be comfortable with them. You may be moving forward or to the rear while executing a side strike during an attack. The strikes and techniques listed are practical and should be the ones you concentrate on. Do not forget the ideas of attacking the attack, cutting through, going into the attack, and balance.

ZEN TIP

If your move is executed in a fancy *manner, it won't be practical. If it is practical, it doesn't have to be* fancy.

SIDE THRUST TO SAME SIDE

This is used to attack the face and abdomen.

STRIKES

Strike to the face.

Strike to the abdomen.

ZEN TIP

Always be sure to sight your target, and make sure your thrust penetrates the target.

ATTACKS

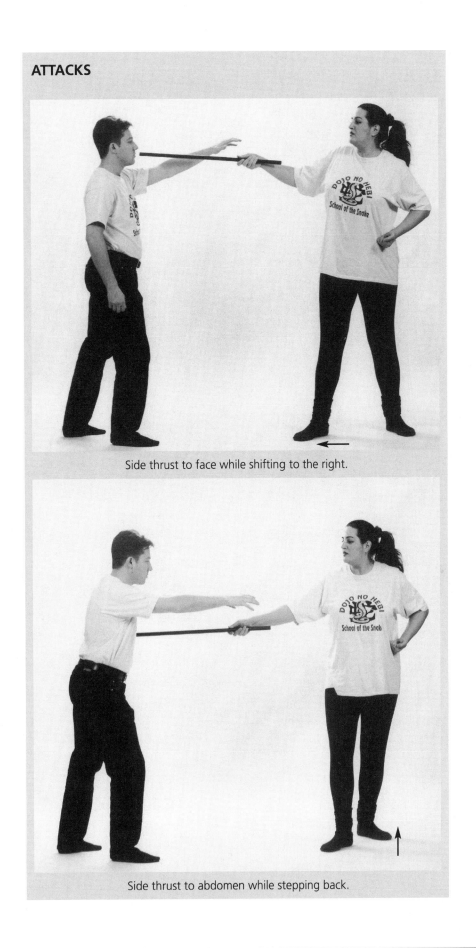

Side thrust to face while shifting to the right.

Side thrust to abdomen while stepping back.

SIDE THRUST TO OPPOSITE SIDE

Striking across the body is the opposite of
the previous strike and attacks the same
targets.

STRIKES

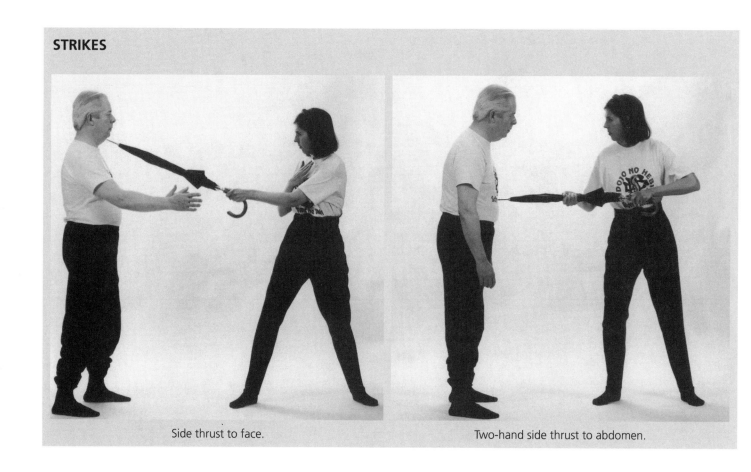

Side thrust to face.

Two-hand side thrust to abdomen.

Ready position.

Reverse side thrust to face while shifting to the right.

Ready position.

Reverse two-hand side abdomen thrust while shifting right.

ZEN TIP

Always look in the direction of your attack.

SIDE OVERHEAD STRIKE
TO SAME SIDE

This targets the attacker's head and shoulders.

STRIKES

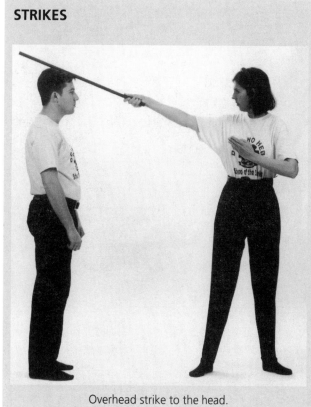

Overhead strike to the head.

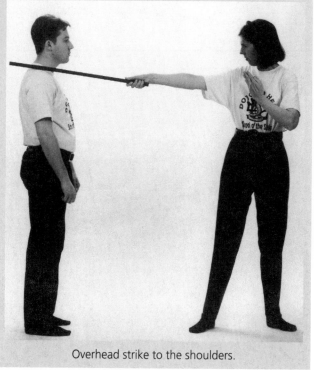

Overhead strike to the shoulders.

Ready position.

Overhead strike to head while shifting away from target.

Ready position.

Two-hand overhead strike to shoulder while shifting in.

Side Strikes and Attacks **67**

SIDE OVERHEAD STRIKE
TO OPPOSITE SIDE

This is the reverse side of the previous strike
and attacks the same targets.

STRIKES

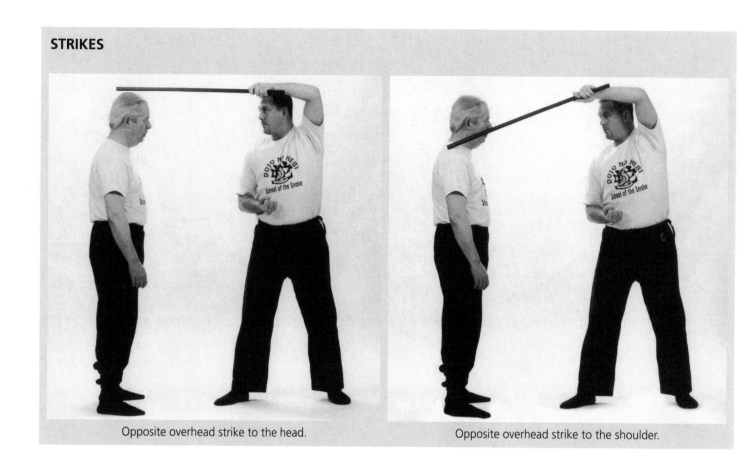

Opposite overhead strike to the head.

Opposite overhead strike to the shoulder.

ZEN TIP

*Maintain an attitude of
going forward regardless of the
direction of the attack.*

Ready position.

Opposite overhead strike to the head while shifting away from the target.

Ready position.

Opposite overhead strike to the shoulder while stepping back.

CROSS BODY STRIKE

This targets the head, ribs, arms, and knees.

When you begin to practice combinations, you will see the value of cutting through rather than slashing at a target. The difference will be obvious when you are changing directions to develop defenses against multiple assailants.

Cross strike to the head.

Cross strike to ribs or arms.

Cross strike to knee.

ATTACKS

Ready position.

Step back and prepare to strike.

Cross strike to head while shifting in.

Ready position.

Cross strike to ribs while shifting in.

Ready position.

Cross strike to knee while shifting in.

10

Rear Strikes and Attacks

No distinction should be made between forward, side, or rear strikes except for the target at which you are aiming. The target is the prime reason for the counterattack, and the target will determine the manner in which you strike when you become aware of your skills. This is based on the amount of practice you put into learning any form of self-defense maneuvers. Continue practicing left-, right-, and two-handed attacks. Maintain the attitudes of going into the attack, attack/no-attack, and cutting through, along with proper balance.

ZEN TIP

Your only concern should be to strike the target with authority and conviction.

BACK THRUST

This is used to attack the middle section of a target behind you. It can also be used to attack the face, which is a difficult target to hit and requires additional practice.

STRIKES

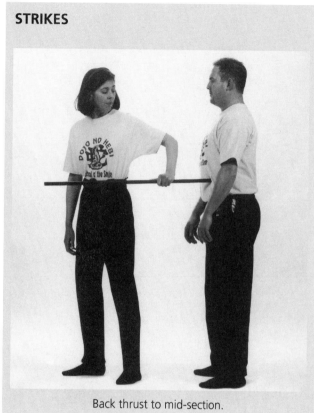

Back thrust to mid-section.

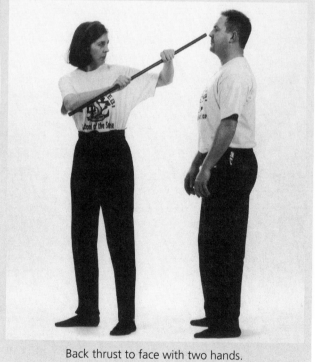

Back thrust to face with two hands.

ATTACKS

Ready position.

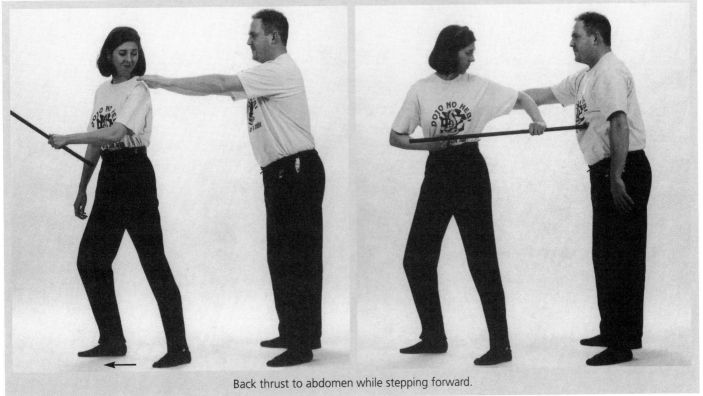

Back thrust to abdomen while stepping forward.

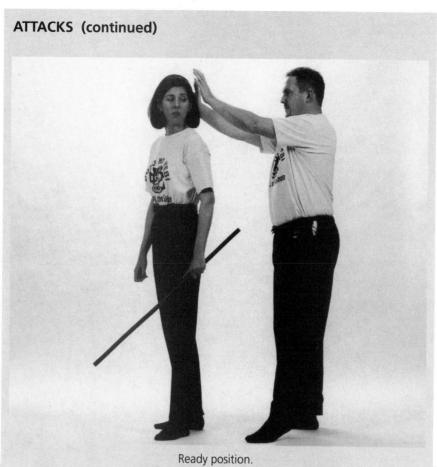

Ready position.

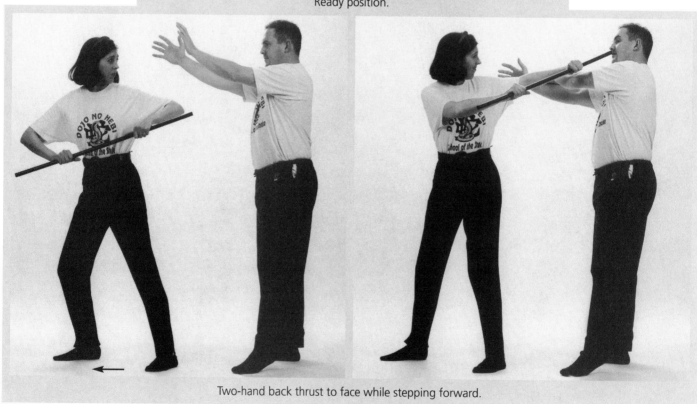

Two-hand back thrust to face while stepping forward.

REAR OVERHEAD STRIKE

Start in the manner of the front overhead
strike (page 47) but continue its arc over
your head. Strike the head or the shoulders
of the target.

STRIKES

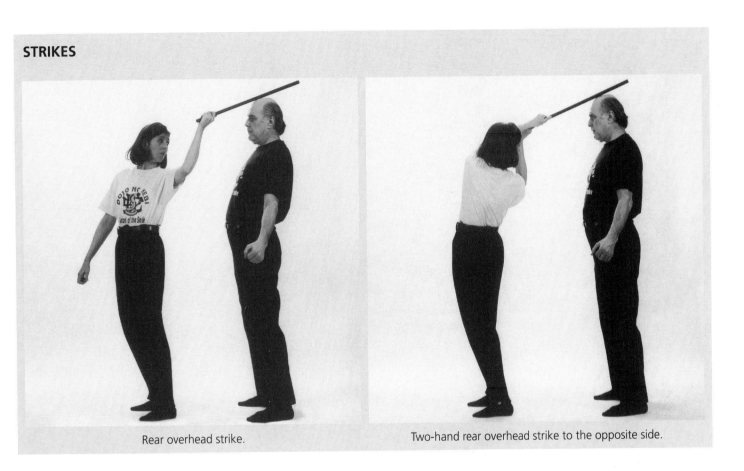

Rear overhead strike.

Two-hand rear overhead strike to the opposite side.

Ready position.

ZEN TIP

Turn your head to see where you are striking the target.

Rear overhead strike to the head while stepping forward.

ATTACKS (continued)

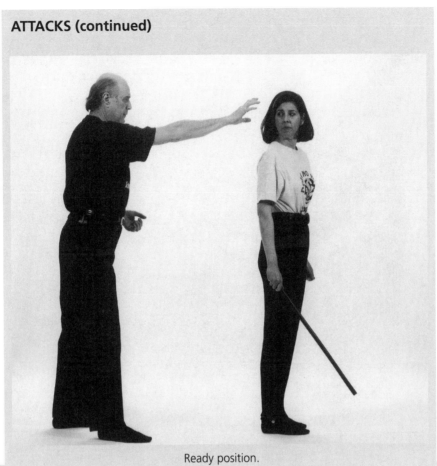

Ready position.

Rear overhead strike with two hands while shifting left and attacking shoulder.

BACKSWING, SAME SIDE

This swing targets the right side of the attacker's head, arms, ribs, and knees.

Backswing to head.

Backswing to ribs or arm.

Backswing to knee.

ATTACKS

Ready position.

Backswing to head while stepping forward.

Ready position.

Backswing to ribs while shifting forward.

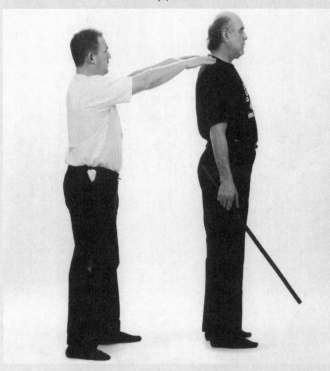

Ready position.

Backswing to knee while stepping back and crouching.

BACKSWING, OPPOSITE SIDE

This attack targets the opposite side of the assailant, striking the head, arms, ribs, and knees.

Be sure to work with the variations of shifting and stepping as you see fit, keeping in mind the practicality of your strikes and attacks. This will enable you to place strikes during attacks where you want them in relation to the body of your opponent.

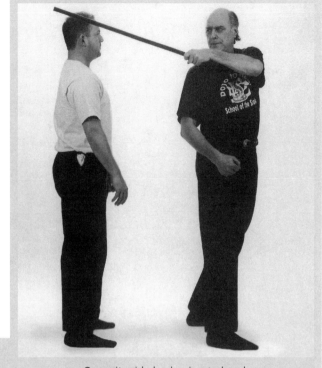

Opposite side backswing to head.

STRIKES

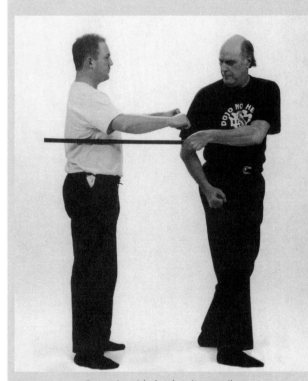

Opposite side backswing to ribs.

Opposite side backswing to knee.

ATTACKS

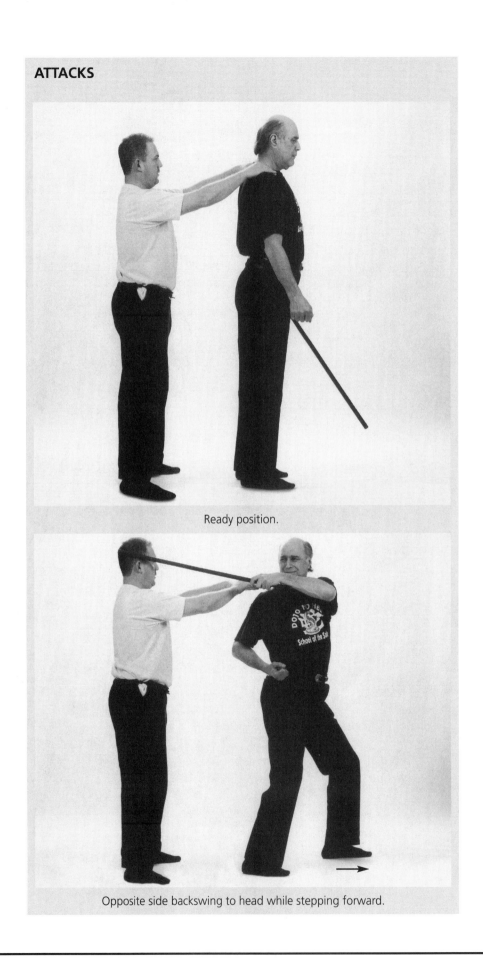

Ready position.

Opposite side backswing to head while stepping forward.

ATTACKS (continued)

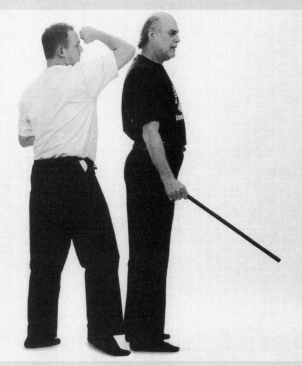

Ready position.

Opposite side backswing to ribs while stepping back.

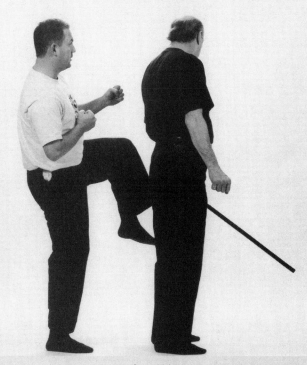

Ready position.

Opposite side backswing to knee while shifting right.

11

Strikes and Attacks in Combination

Seasoned warriors rely to a great extent on their ability to execute techniques in combinations that will ensure their victory. They practice with an attitude that enables them to gain more control with their chosen weapon and to use it with more sophistication. In many instances, they develop elegance as an aspect of their technique. *Elegance* is defined as grace, poise, and a flowing of action with ease. Think of elegance as essential to proper technique.

As with everything else, there are countless combinations. After you have mastered those shown in this book, endeavor to develop your own style. This is the true Zen idea: to become one with your weapon and understand its properties—all to your advantage. It is the meaning of the saying, "The sword is the soul of the samurai." This state of mind can only be attained through constant practice.

ZEN TIP

Walk away. Always walk away—if you can.

In addition, developing fluidity in motion is also an aspect of the idea of going into the target. This is the meaning of elegance. The attitude of attack/no-attack becomes logical when you see the control you have over an enemy once you learn to wield your weapon correctly.

We live in a stress-ridden society. It is to your advantage to stay alert to what is going on around you since you might have to protect yourself and your loved ones both mentally and physically. The physical aspect of self-defense should only be used as a last resort. It is always easier to walk away from a situation regardless of the conditions that seem to prevail. It should also be understood that when you have to deal with a situation, do only what is necessary, without losing control and beating someone into oblivion even though they may deserve it.

There should be no distinction of importance between your application of techniques. A straight thrust is as valid as a rear thrust or a side overhead strike.

TWO-PART COMBINATION NUMBER 1

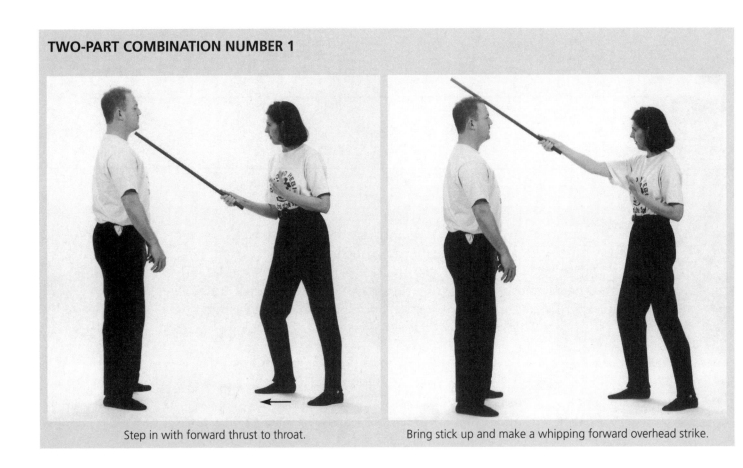

Step in with forward thrust to throat.

Bring stick up and make a whipping forward overhead strike.

TWO-PART COMBINATION NUMBER 2

Shifting left with two-hand middle thrust.

Switching to left hand and forward outside strike.

TWO-PART COMBINATION NUMBER 3

Step forward with same side rear overhead.

Step back with two-hand rear thrust.

TWO-PART COMBINATION NUMBER 4

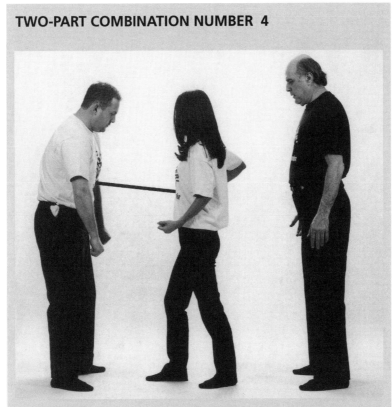

Step forward with abdomen thrust.

Turn 180 degrees to the rear with reverse forward overhead strike.

TWO-PART COMBINATION NUMBER 5

Step in with forward overhead.

Execute two-hand front thrust.

TWO-PART COMBINATION NUMBER 6

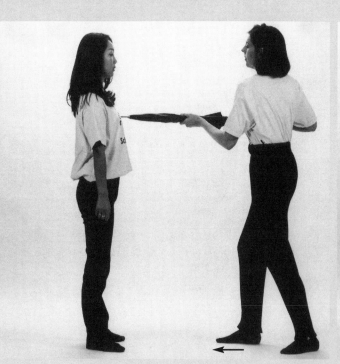

Step forward with two-hand thrust to chest.

Step forward with two-hand thrust to abdomen.

THREE-PART COMBINATION NUMBER 1

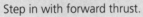

Step in with forward thrust.

Turn right with rear overhead.

Shift left with front overhead.

THREE-PART COMBINATION NUMBER 2

Attack to right with two-hand thrust.

Two-hand wide-grip forward outside strike.

Two-hand wide-grip back thrust.

THREE-PART COMBINATION NUMBER 3

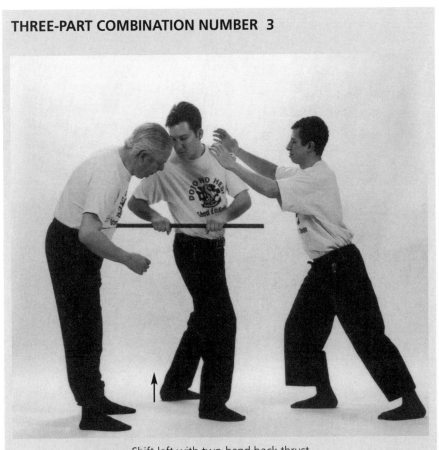

Shift left with two-hand back thrust.

Step in with two-hand forward thrust.

Step back with reverse rear over shoulder.

THREE-PART COMBINATION NUMBER 4

Step forward and execute front rising strike to groin.

Step back and to the rear and execute overhead strike.

Forward downward thrust.

THREE-PART COMBINATION NUMBER 5

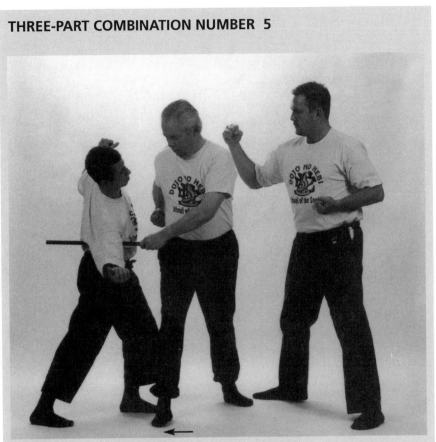

Step back opposite side backswing.

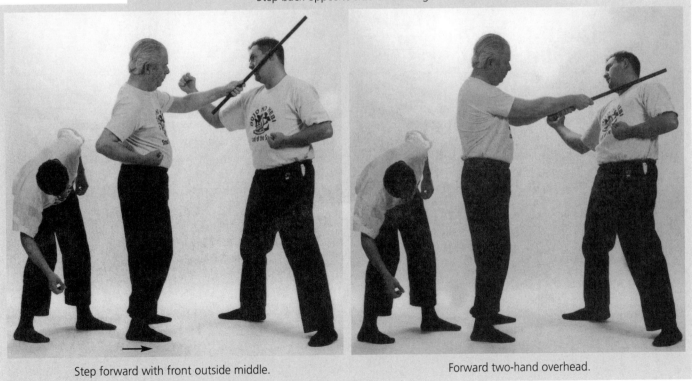

Step forward with front outside middle.

Forward two-hand overhead.

Shift right with reverse overhead to left side.

Same hand rear backswing.

Two-hand forward thrust to abdomen.

FOUR-PART, FIVE-PART, AND MORE COMBINATIONS

Now it is your turn to invent combinations that you personally will be comfortable with. Take any of the two- or three-part combinations and add the next element of your choosing. This will enable you to develop additional attributes of your own technique. You are purposely left to your own imagination in the anticipation that you will proceed to develop your skills.

ZEN TIP

If you are executing with correct attitude and intention, two or three strikes are enough to disable a single attacker.

12
Deflections, Not Blocks

Deflections are essential for defending against many types of attacks, but they should not be considered requisite at all times. That is why this chapter is placed after the attacking and combination chapters. You should know and practice deflections but should not rely on them to stop an attack. Attacks are stopped with forward, side, and rear strikes in combination.

Deflections enable you to move into an attack quickly and to deliver your countermeasures with more effectiveness. Deflections are *not* blocks! The difference between a deflection and a block is the intention of its use. If you meet force with force, as with a block, you are relying on strength or clever technique to overcome the opposition. This creates unnecessary conflict. When you deflect and divert incoming energy, it is easier to deliver a counterattack without restriction. This is a subtle point that must be understood if you are to become efficient. When properly executed, a defensive move consists of a deflection and strike done as one continuous movement. Once you learn the deflections, strive to use them in all of your techniques.

ZEN TIP

Deflect, don't block. In time you will use deflections as part of the entire attack sequence.

THE THREE COMMON DEFLECTIONS

High Deflections

High deflections protect against attacks to the upper body and head. Observe the angle of the stick—the tip is pointed downward. This permits anything coming in to slide down and away, giving you the advantage when executing a retaliatory strike. If you hold the stick straight, with no angle, you will have to bear the brunt of the entire attack while absorbing the weight of the arm or device being used against you, which could be considered a block. If you hold the stick point up, an incoming object or fist can slide down the shaft into your hand, causing injury.

Incorrect—straight.

Incorrect—tip up.

Correct—tip down.

HIGH DEFLECTIONS AGAINST ATTACKS

Ready position.

Deflecting a punch while stepping back.

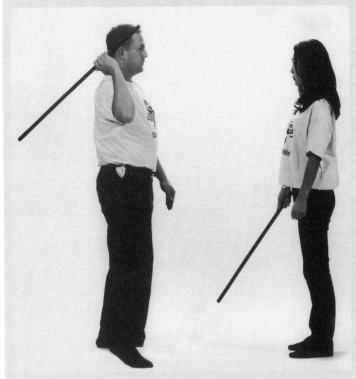

Ready position.

Deflecting a stick while stepping in.

Low Deflections

Low deflections protect the legs and lower abdomen from kicks or other weapons. Never attempt to reach for the attacking kick or weapon by leaning in. Let the attacker present his or her intentions.

LOW DEFLECTION

Incorrect.

Correct.

LOW DEFLECTIONS AGAINST ATTACKS

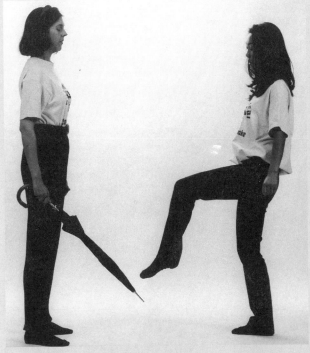

Ready position.

Defending against a kick while stepping back.

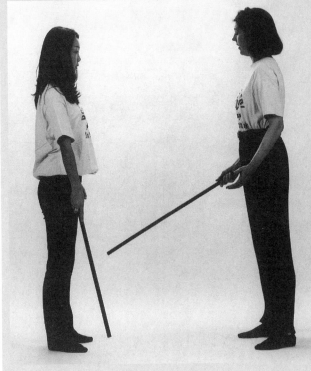

Ready position.

Defending against a stick while stepping in.

Middle Deflections

Middle outside and middle inside deflections protect the midsection. When deflecting from the right side with the right arm and going to the left, it is an *outside* move. When using your right arm toward the right, it is an *inside* move. The same applies to the left arm and side.

MIDDLE OUTSIDE DEFLECTIONS

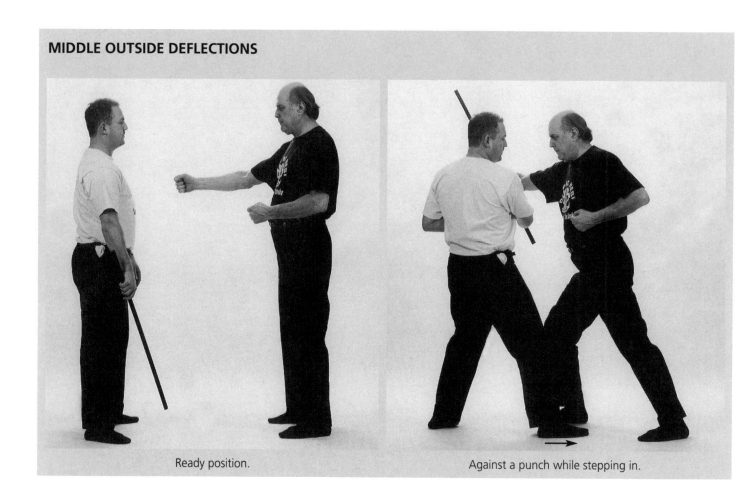

Ready position.

Against a punch while stepping in.

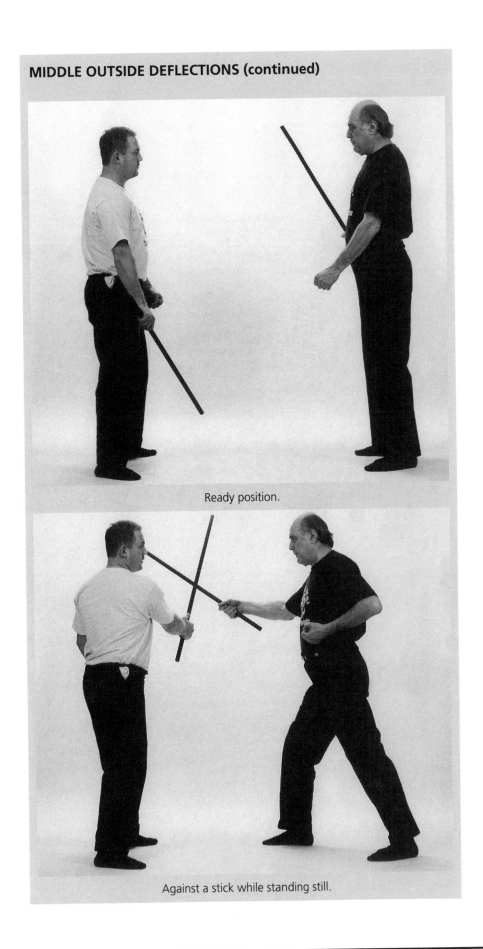

Ready position.

Against a stick while standing still.

Ready position.

Against a punch while shifting left.

Ready position.

Against a stick while stepping back.

13

Self-Defense with a
Stick, Cane, or Umbrella

Self-defense is comprised of fundamental actions used by an
individual to protect him- or herself with sensible and controlled
techniques. In this chapter you will learn to act with a deflection
and a strike as one maneuver. All of the devices—a stick, cane, or
umbrella—will be used in the examples. Get used to the idea of not
relying on any particular device. As in the previous chapters, not
everything can be shown. Your repertoire will increase based on
your amount of practice. Practice until your stick, cane, or umbrella
is a part of you.

ZEN TIP

*There is no such thing as
"fair" fighting.*

DEFLECTIONS AND STRIKES

A PUNCH IS AIMED AT YOUR HEAD

Ready position.

Step back with high deflection.

Forward outside strike to ribs.

Ready position.

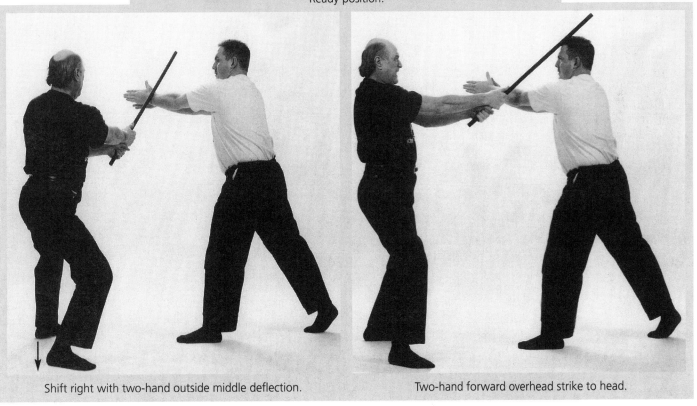

Shift right with two-hand outside middle deflection.

Two-hand forward overhead strike to head.

A KICK IS AIMED AT YOUR GROIN

Ready position.

Shift right with low deflection.

Front rising strike to groin.

SIDE PUSH FROM LEFT

Ready position.

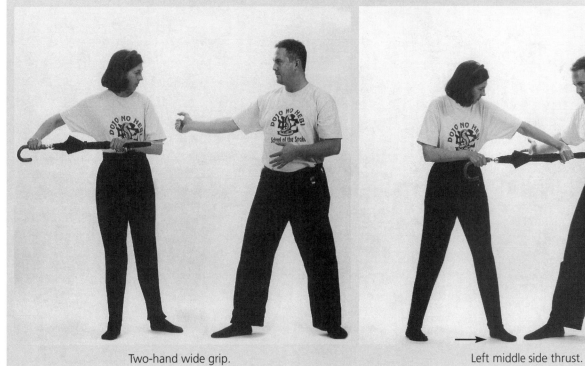

Two-hand wide grip.

Left middle side thrust.

REAR GRAB AND FRONT PUNCH

Ready position.

Two-hand forward thrust.

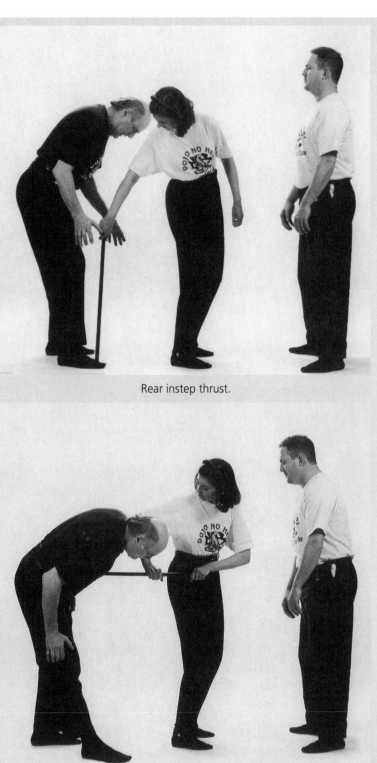

Rear instep thrust.

Two-hand rear thrust.

GRABBED FROM BEHIND IN A CHOKE HOLD

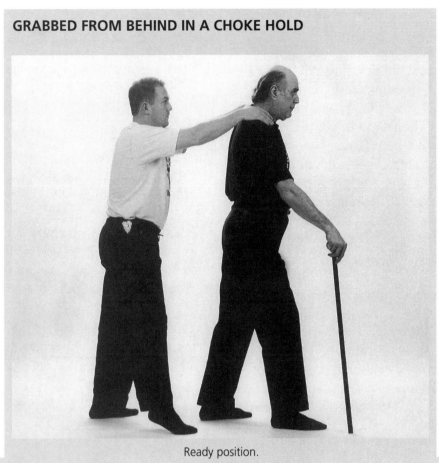

Ready position.

Two-hand back thrust to face.

Turn 180 degrees with forward reverse to head.

As your efforts begin to show results, you will find that certain techniques work more smoothly. This is because your body works in its own way and cannot be compared to someone else's. The examples given indicate fundamental defenses against common attacks, but they should not be considered the ultimate or only methods. There is no such thing as the ultimate method, and no *style* is more effective than any other, regardless of the culture from which it emanates. The only thing that really matters is your desire to succeed in your endeavor. Do not expect the *style* to be the winner in a challenge.

The amount of time, effort, and energy you put into developing your skills will directly affect your level of skill. Have the heart to succeed and apply all of your energy and effort. Otherwise, the skills you practice will be little more than simple dance steps to amuse your friends. *Zen and the Art of Stickfighting* gives you all the tools that are needed

Zen Tip

Put your heart into what you do, or you will not attain the true measure of your intent.

to become stronger and more positive in your approach to self-defense and every other aspect of your life.

Practice and develop your own ideas. They are as valid as anything else is. Once you understand the basics, the development of any art depends upon your desire to master it.

Zen Tip

You can only fight the way you practice.

14

Self-Defense Against Weapons and Multiple Attackers

You will have no problem dealing with dangerous situations involving weapon attacks if you have maintained your practice with a serious attitude.

Though knives, sticks, and bottles can be thrown at you, the ability to counter an attack with intelligent strategy is still functional. An attack with a gun suggests that you are in range of the weapon, and your quickness, though assured with constant practice, is no match for the velocity (300 to 900 meters per second) that a bullet moves toward a target at any range. Therefore, moves intended to defend against guns are omitted.

ZEN TIP

With a stick, cane, or umbrella, you always have an advantage in reach. Use this advantage to your advantage.

STICK AGAINST STICK

HEAD ATTACK

Ready position.

Step in with a rising deflection.

Switch hands and execute forward outside strike to head.

THRUST ATTACK TO MIDDLE

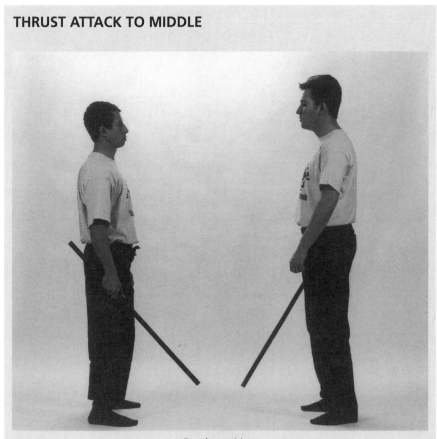

Ready position.

Step back with middle outside deflection.

Execute forward reverse strike.

Ready position.

Shift back with low deflection.

Step in with two-hand forward thrust.

ZEN TIP

Do not lean forward or reach in for the attacker's weapon.

RIB ATTACK

Ready position.

Shift right with middle outside deflection.

Forward outside strike to knee.

STICK AGAINST KNIFE OR CHAIN

Of all types of attacks, those with knives and chains are the most frightening. Endeavor to maintain your presence of mind, and will yourself not to feel terrorized should this situation occur. Practice with the idea that your weapon—a stick, cane, or umbrella— can successfully and adequately protect you. Continue to train with more authority and conviction. In these tactics, quick and fast responses are essential and may be executed without deflections.

> ## ZEN TIP
>
> *Continue to execute thrusts to the eyes and abdomen until you are comfortable with the tactic.*

SLASHING ATTACK TO YOUR FACE

Ready position.

Step back and execute a forward thrust to the eyes.

Execute forward thrust to the abdomen.

THRUST ATTACK TO STOMACH

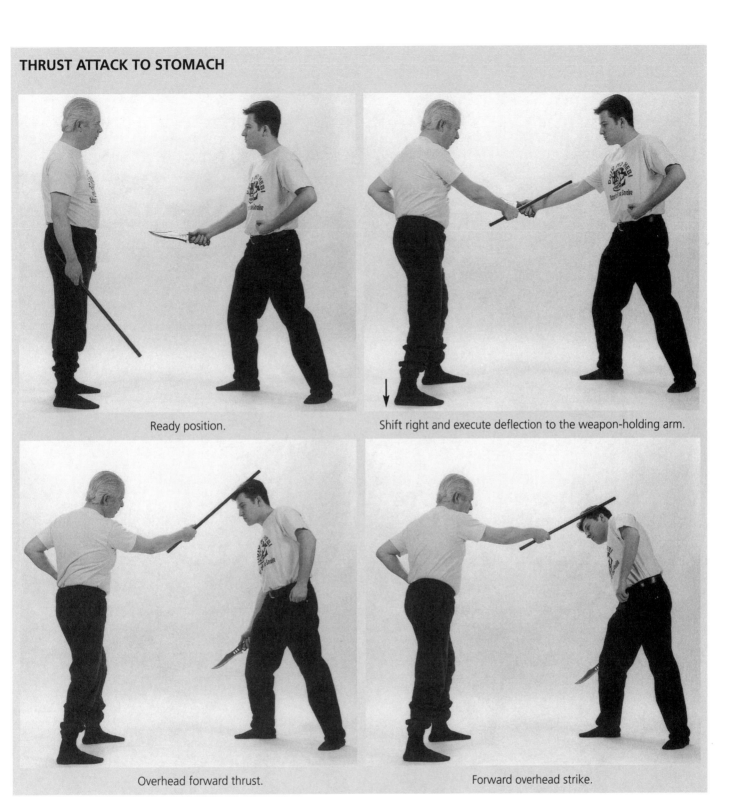

Ready position.

Shift right and execute deflection to the weapon-holding arm.

Overhead forward thrust.

Forward overhead strike.

ZEN TIP

Do not strike at the weapon.

UPWARD RIPPING ATTACK WITH KNIFE

Ready position.

Two-hand low deflection.

Step forward with wide two-hand thrust to face.

Two-hand forward overhead strike.

SWINGING CHAIN ATTACK

Shift left with two-hand middle deflection.

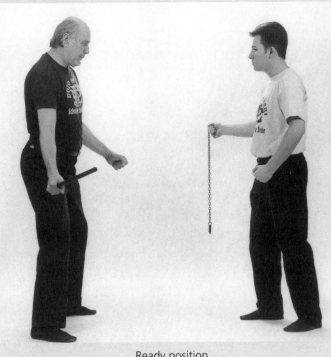

Ready position.

Shift right with two-hand forward thrust.

Zen Tip

Use visualization and see yourself perfecting techniques.

STICK AGAINST MULTIPLE ASSAILANTS

When defending against multiple assailants, maintain the attitude of dealing with one attacker at a time. Use whatever tactics are necessary, in the same manner as if you were dealing with any other type of attack. Keep in mind that with a stick, cane, or umbrella, you are armed and have the ability to protect yourself without excessive fear of being hurt.

**TWO UNARMED ATTACKERS
APPROACH FROM BOTH SIDES**

Ready position.

Two-hand right-side thrust.

TWO UNARMED ATTACKERS APPROACH
FROM BOTH SIDES (continued)

Two-hand left-side thrust.

Single hand overhead right strike.

Side outside head strike to left.

TWO UNARMED ATTACKERS COME
FROM FRONT AND BACK

Ready position.

Step in with forward thrust.

Rear overhead strike.

Forward outside strike.

TWO UNARMED ATTACKERS COME FROM THE FRONT AND ONE FROM THE REAR

Ready position.

Shift back with two-hand rear thrust.

Lean forward with two-hand forward thrust.

Shift right with two-hand side thrust.

The tactics shown are only representative examples of what can be done in the given situations. You are restricted only by your own imagination. Once you are able to execute the tactics being shown confidently, you will be comfortable developing your own tactics.

15

A Formal Exercise

Practicing formal exercises is essential if you wish to gain mastery in any art form. In music, a student practices scales. In the martial arts, the exercises are called *kata*. Kata are prescribed movements that train a student to become skillful with techniques while assisting in the development and fun of advanced improvisational practice routines.

The following series of sequences uses simple patterns in combined form to develop advanced skills. In time, you should work through all of the sequences as extensions of each other until the kata is performed as one move. Consider it a dance with a stick. You might want to listen to your favorite music while doing the kata and work within the constraints of the rhythm you are hearing. Once you are familiar with the recommended routine, feel free to work with any deflection and countermeasure as long as it does not throw you off balance or interfere with the proper execution of technique. Become proficient and maintain your comfort during the entire kata. Breathe where it is necessary, and maintain the attitudes of cutting through and going into the attack.

BASIC STICKFIGHTING KATA

STANDING IN THE READY POSITION, HOLD THE STICK WITH A WIDE TWO-HAND GRIP. STEP 90 DEGREES TO THE LEFT WHILE EXECUTING A LOW DEFLECTION AND IMMEDIATELY CONVERT TO A RISING DEFLECTION.

Ready position with wide two-hand grip.

Step left 90 degrees.

Execute a low deflection.

Convert to rising deflection.

STEPPING FORWARD WITH THE RIGHT FOOT, GRASP STICK OVERHEAD WITH TWO HANDS. SWITCH TO THE RIGHT HAND AND EXECUTE A FRONT OUTSIDE STRIKE.

Bring feet together and grasp stick with both hands.

Step in with right-hand overhead strike.

Continue with forward outside strike.

TURNING 180 DEGREES TO THE RIGHT, FACING IN THE OPPOSITE DIRECTION, EXECUTE A LOW DEFLECTION FOLLOWED BY A RISING DEFLECTION, BOTH WITH THE RIGHT HAND.

Turn 180 degrees to the right.

Execute a low deflection.

Convert to rising deflection.

STEPPING IN WITH THE LEFT FOOT, GRASP STICK OVERHEAD WITH TWO HANDS. SWITCH THE STICK TO YOUR LEFT HAND AND EXECUTE A FRONT OUTSIDE STRIKE. THIS IS THE MIRROR IMAGE OF THE SEQUENCE ON PAGE 133.

Bring feet together and grasp stick with both hands.

Step in with left-hand overhead strike.

Continue with forward outside strike.

TURN LEFT 90 DEGREES WITH LEFT LOW AND RISING DEFLECTIONS AS ONE CONTINUOUS MOVE.

Turn 90 degrees left.

Execute left-hand low deflection.

Convert to rising deflection.

STEPPING FORWARD WITH RIGHT LEG, SWITCH HANDS IN OVERHEAD POSITION AND EXECUTE RIGHT LOW AND HIGH DEFLECTIONS.

Bring feet together and grasp stick overhead with both hands.

Step forward with right leg and execute right low deflection.

Convert to rising deflection.

STEP FORWARD WITH LEFT LEG, SWITCH HANDS TO OVERHEAD POSITION, AND EXECUTE LEFT LOW AND RISING DEFLECTIONS.

Bring feet together and grasp stick overhead with both hands.

Step forward with left leg and execute left low deflection.

Convert to rising deflection.

STEP FORWARD WITH RIGHT LEG, SWITCH TO TWO-HAND GRIP, AND EXECUTE TWO-HAND OVERHEAD STRIKE, FOLLOWED BY A TWO-HAND FORWARD THRUST.

Bring feet together and grasp stick overhead with both hands.

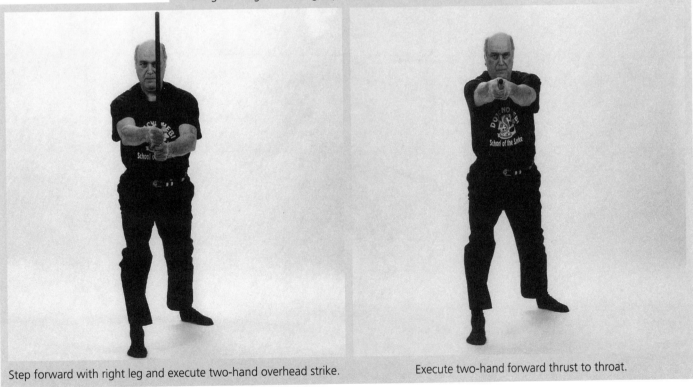

Step forward with right leg and execute two-hand overhead strike.

Execute two-hand forward thrust to throat.

STEP 90 DEGREES RIGHT WITH LOW RIGHT DEFLECTION.

Step 90 degrees right with two-hand grip.

Execute low right deflection.

EXECUTE A RIGHT FORWARD THRUST. SWITCH HANDS AND EXECUTE LEFT OUTSIDE MIDDLE STRIKE. THIS IS ALL FROM THE SAME POSITION.

Execute right-hand forward thrust.

Bring left foot up together with two-hand grip.

Step forward with left outside middle strike.

TURN 180 DEGREES TO THE OPPOSITE DIRECTION WITH LEFT LOW DEFLECTION.

Grasp stick with both hands and turn 180 degrees to the opposite direction.

Execute left-hand low deflection.

EXECUTE A LEFT FORWARD THRUST. SWITCH HANDS AND EXECUTE A RIGHT OUTSIDE MIDDLE STRIKE. AGAIN, THIS IS ALL FROM THE SAME POSITION.

Execute left-hand forward thrust.

Bring feet together with two-hand grip.

Execute right outside middle strike.

TURN LEFT 90 DEGREES WHILE EXECUTING LEFT MIDDLE INSIDE DEFLECTION. EXECUTE LEFT THRUST TO MIDDLE. THOUGH YOU ARE FACING TOWARD THE REAR, THE PICTURES ARE SHOWN HEAD-ON.

Turn left 90 degrees with left middle inside deflection.

Execute left-hand middle thrust.

STEP IN RIGHT, SWITCHING TO RIGHT HAND, AND EXECUTE A REVERSE STRIKE TO THE HEAD.

Step in right, grasping stick with both hands.

Switch to right hand.

Execute right reverse strike to head.

STEP FORWARD, SWITCH TO TWO-HAND OVERHEAD POSITION, AND EXECUTE A TWO-HAND OVERHEAD STRIKE. STEP IN WITH A TWO-HAND FORWARD MIDDLE THRUST.

Grasp stick with both hands overhead.

Execute two-hand overhead strike.

Execute two-hand middle thrust.

STEP BACK TURNING 180 DEGREES (FACING FRONT) WITH WIDE TWO-HAND GRIP, AND EXECUTE LEFT-SIDE MIDDLE THRUST.

Step back 180 degrees with wide two-hand grip.

Shift left and execute left-side middle thrust.

SHIFT RIGHT WITH WIDE TWO-HAND GRIP, AND EXECUTE RIGHT-SIDE MIDDLE THRUST.

Shift right with wide two-hand grip.

Execute right-side middle thrust.

Step back to starting position.

It is important to complete the entire kata as one unified series of moves. The basis of kata is to develop your skills using the techniques shown but, more importantly, to develop the ability to work your attacks with comfort and ease. When practicing kata, imagine yourself surrounded by enemies. Make kata as real as possible.

Afterword

What you have been taught in this book is an introduction to Zen and the art of stickfighting. Along with the techniques, the Zen Tips are essentially common sense, and their wisdom should be contemplated.

It is appreciated that those of you who have gone through the rigorous training and discipline of stickfighting will use it intelligently for the purposes it is intended and not as an aggressive tool for intimidation.

Should your safety be compromised or your life be threatened, then by all means use what you have learned in the appropriate manner. As with all methods of self-defense, the practitioner should make sure that no other avenue of disengagement is possible. Even when there seems to be no alternative, it is urged that you try to alleviate matters without getting into a physical confrontation.

Masters of martial arts practice their skills day in and day out for many years, and the vast majority of true masters can earnestly report that they have never had to use any of their skills. When you truly know who and what you are, you don't have to worry about defining it for anyone—and you certainly never have to show it off in an attempt to gain recognition.